PARENTING

Are We doing the Best We Can?

The question Are We doing the Best We Can?
To educate, raise and protect our youth.
Our youth are Our Future; we need to do everything we can to save them.
Examine Our Communication, Conversation, Interaction,
and Support with Our Children and Youth.

RONALD FRANCIS

To order additional copies of this book, contact:
Xlibris
844-714-8691
www.Xlibris.com
Orders@Xlibris.com

ISBN: Softcover   978-1-6698-5715-0
       EBook   978-1-6698-5714-3

Library of Congress Control Number: 2022921832

Print information available on the last page

Rev. date: 12/02/2022

I pose these questions, due to the increase of crime and murders being committed by our youth. Some crimes are being committed by youth under eighteen.

Why are our youth (12-16 years old) in the streets 12am thru 6am.

Where are the parents? They all can't be sneaking out the house, without someone knowing. Majority of Baby Boomers and Millennials were in the house by 8-9pm.

No Child ever ran or controlled the house, which was paid for by the Parents / Adults.

The youth were raised and taught to respect one another, especially their parents and adults.

We are the Parents We take the Lead. We have the responsibility to give guidance, love and understanding.

A child is not supposed to raise themselves. There are some circumstances where there is one parent working long hour or even two jobs; we have a responsibility to our youth.

We brought them into this world. We need to make time for them.

Our responsibility is to give our youth a better start in life through education, help, and encouragement. I call it an Investment. The Investment is seeing your child (children) develop and utilize their full potential. See them grow into wise, productive citizens, Leaders, Prominent Individuals.

Do we have expectations for our children? Do we let them know our expectations?

Parents

We are all Role Models to someone.

Are we helping our youth?

Are we having regular conversation with them?

What are their concerns, or worries?

Friends cannot replace / or be a replacement for parent connection.

Quality Time

Do we set time aside at Breakfast, Dinner, take walks or just have a special family night? Are we paying attention to what our children are saying verbally – emotionally?

Our Youth / Your Child Needs Attention.

You need to be there for them First, before they seek others for advice, directions, and leadership.

Each generation is different, but there are common denominators, love, and understanding.

I think television and especially video games (dating myself) have taken most of our time.

How many conversations have we had recently?

Do we talk about their future?

Do we talk to them about family history, struggles and success stories?

Some of Our Family history has been lost through generation.

Some have been blessed to have good accurate history of their family.

I believe if our youth knew their history, family accomplishments and history their family may have been involved in, it would build their self-esteem.

They would stand strong knowing anything is possible and can be achieved.

Before you know it, your child –children will be an adolescent then an adult.

Time goes fast. Enjoy every moment, birth, birthday, celebration, game, graduation and performance.

We have enough people belittling, demeaning, bulling individuals, they certainly do not need to hear or get it from those who love them and have their best interest.

Do we make them feel important; praise them when they do well, and great accomplishments.

Try to avoid negativity; Do not cause resentment

Encourage and support, help homework assignments, projects, and athletic practices.

Do they feel capable to succeed, and worthy of compliments.

You know your child better, than anyone and everyone else. Trust your instincts.

Behavior (watch behavior)

Boundaries (are there boundaries)

Limits (are there limits)

Guidance (do we instruct them)

Support (do we support them)

Remember our children are watching us, from your mannerisms, behavior and to your response to issues and circumstances.

Our youth have to be reminded, understand and distinguish between movies, shows, and reality.

Fatherhood

There seems to be a lack of Fathers involved in our youth's life.

A child is not a Trophy, put on a table and walk away, to brag about how many children you have fathered.

The important part of a father, that you are engaged, involved, and committed to your child / children's.

One of the special rewards, is you both can learn from each other and have enjoyable memories and moments.

There is no excuse for slacking off your responsibility. We all know two things happen as you get older and your health declines and you review your life.

Do you have any regrets? Do you want to make amends? Could you have done better?

What happens when you child or their children want to know you or they become very successful then you want to a part of their life.

<u>Grandparents</u>

Are a Blessing, they give wise information; they are witty, they may not have All the answers but can lead you the right way.

Grandparents are lifesavers, babysitters, listeners, supporters-enforcers, mediators, and great cooks and have great food and love to go out.

Children also keep grandparents mentally, and physically sharp.

Questions / Thoughts

What can we do as parents to ensure our youth will be able to LIVE and Excel in life?

Find things that peak their interest, their attention in a good way.

What can we do, to pass on our experiences, to help them know we all may have passed some of those road blocks they are facing today. Distractions, Temptations, peer pressure, someone to listen, give advice, and positive input.

Thoughts

Do we pass on the values we were taught as children and young adults?

One of the Biggest things is RESPECT for life, for others and yourself.

Again previously mentioned do our youth represent us, Minnie ME's.

Do they react to issues the same way you do.

What Trails have you shown or displayed

Respect

Honesty

Kindness

Communication

Have we forgotten to continually emphasize to Think?

Common Sense cannot be left behind.

Common Sense should tell you Right from Wrong.

It seems individuals are living, responding to situations on emotions, trying to impress rather than use reasoning.

The word consequence continually is mentioned, because it carries a lot of weight.

Qualities

Patience

Leadership

Humility

Accountability

Honesty

Respectfulness

Motivation

Confidence

Discipline

Self-Control

Morals

I looked up Morals and Values to reassure that I had the right definition.

Morals are learned characteristics, rules, right from wrong.

Values are set of principles inherit, individual learned.

I believe some of our youth's morals have be challenged,

Some have may have been taught right and wrong or the consequences.

I believe some of our youth need to be reminded; everyone needs values. Everyone has families and they need to be respected.

I keep emphasizing Respect, because everyday citizens, neighbors, babies, seniors have been killed for nothing.

Life has a meaning, there is no-RESET Button on Life, and it's not a game.

Some blame television, games, and other entertainment.

You don't have look at some of these things; you have to be able to distinguish what's not true and reality.

Respect

The Importance of Respect must be taught.

Respect for others and the Respect for others property.

Respect yourself, you are important, your life matters. Part of that means to carry yourself in a respectful way, thinking about your actions.

Establish yourself in life, make your own mark, and follow your desires.

Responsibilities

I believe parents responsibilities are:

Provide –for your child

Nurturing- helping to develop

Protect –from any harm

Guidance- help understand this world, and life.

Encourage-to be your best at all times, it might not be easy, but try.

Respect- teaches them to respect you and others, and their property.

Be there for them.

After working with several youth groups, I noticed parent support is a very important factor.

Taking your child to practice, games, and programs and be there with them learning, growing, discussing, and celebrating Together. Not just dropping them off and come back later.

Challenges

Today more of our youth are experiencing many challenges.

Young people go through a lot of emotions, worry, anxiety, and pressure.

They need guidance, we need to be there for them and if needed get help for them from professionals.

We know our children. It's better to check on them now, than experience issues later.

Hold on to your Values.

Morals, what is right and wrong.

Our youth have to think about their Actions. Their actions can affect many.

There are Actions and there are Consequences.

When you break the Law there is going to be consequences.

When our youth are with social groups or circles, remind them they do not have to follow or participate. They do not have to impress or follow what others are doing.

There are some unhappy, frustrated, hateful individuals in the world, remember the Old Saying Misery Loves Company.

If they feel uncomfortable walk away from any situation, no one will think less of them.

Everyone has been born with unique qualities.

Our youth should want to be the best.

Crime

There has been an increase of crime and murders.

There is a lack of Respect for life; Lack of Remorse, and disregard for the law.

There are Senseless murders over short patience, disputes, arguments, hatred, or someone wanting to hurt others. If we can stop, step back a minute and THINK.

Is it worth it?

I believe some of these actions may stem from the lack of guidance, love, and understanding.

We are All Feed Up, disturbed, Frustrated hearing killing of kids, young adults and seniors for no apparent reason.

We all have the responsibility to do what we can to help each other

The actions you take affect others, your family and other families.

Games, videos, and some television shows are not reality.

This Book is meant to encourage Parents to continual press to make a difference in your child's life. Many don't need a reminder; some may need to make notes. There is always something or someone you can learn from.

With life's up and downs and pivots we need to remember the gifts we have and how blessed we are; family and friends are the only things we have on this earth.

Let's make sure they know it.

Conclusion

It's true the Pandemic has brought out the worst of some; due to lack of jobs, education, and money.

There is a lot of work to done.

Let's start with our home.

Let's invest in our youth. We cannot give up on them or believe there's no hope.

Together we can find ways to encourage and help them with their desires, hopes, and careers. Parents are the First Line of Contact.

Newspaper Article

Think! Your Life Depends On It

by Ron Francis

Young brothers, take a minute to think about what you are doing to each other. I'm concerned about our race.

We, as Black men are slowing declining, either by death or incarceration. The freedom our forefathers died for is to no avail if we don't build on their positive contributions.

Life is too short and you can accomplish whatever you want with patience, perserverance, and the right direction. The right direction is "Faith in God." You can't find faith in alcohol and drugs, and fast money. If we keep killing our race, there won't be any Black men left,

"No one to love and guide" our women and children.

We have many Black role models that we can emulate, and learn from, other than just "Sports Figures." Remember, Blacks have always been prominent inventors, doctors, politicians and writers.

Take a minute to think! Is killing a person worth it? Two Families are Destroyed. One family member is dead. One family member goes to jail. If you care about your Family, Parents, Children, Girlfriend, you'll think!

Think Now before it's too late.

Think Now before you'll have lots of time to think (Incarceration).

Freedom. Opportunity. Achievement. Tranquility. Faith. Perserverance . . .

(Ron Francis lives in Yeadon, Pennsylvania.)

To the Editor:

Back in 1995, I wrote the following opinion piece for the Philadelphia New Observer.

"Young brothers, take a minute to think about what you are doing to each other. I'm concerned about our race. We black men are slowly declining, either by death or incarceration. The freedom our forefathers died for is of no avail if we don't build on their positive contributions,

"Life is too short and you can accomplish whatever you want with patience, perseverance, and the right direction. That right direction is faith in God. You can't find faith in alcohol and drugs and fast money. If we keep killing our race, there won't be any Black men left – no one to love and guide our women and children.

"We have many Black role models to emulate and learn from – other than just sport figures. Blacks have been prominent inventors, doctors, politicians and writers.

"Take a minute and think! Is killing another person worth it? Two families are destroyed: in one, a family member is dead; in the other, a family member goes to jail.

"Think now before it's too late; Think now before now before you have lots more time to think about it when you're incarcerated. Think: Freedom, Opportunity, Achievement, Tranquility, Faith, and Perseverance

I believe these thoughts still hold true today...life is a precious gift. We all have special and creative gifts that can shared with others. Hopefully our youth will understand the struggles that make it possible for them fulfill their dreams.

—Ron Francis
(Ron Francis retires shortly after a 40-year career in the military and Veterans Administration)

Additional Information

Mother

A Mother's Love is there from
Beginning to the end.
A Mother is a friend, Conferee,
And a Teacher.
A Mother can feel your hurt, your pain,
your Enthusiasm, and Your Love.
A Mother Shares her Life Long Experiences,
Knowledge, and her Sentiments.
A Mother Encourages You to be the best
You can be, And Stands Behind You.
A Mother's Devotion and Unselfishness
Can Never be replaced, or Repaid.

MOTHER, Thank You
For All The Above!

Mothers Day

Is

Everyday

More than an influence in the life of a child she's an

Ointment from God on her offspring so mild

Tender sweet touch calming, Tender young tears show a

Heart full of Love bathing each with her tears an

Rewarded by God for such heavenly Love

THANK GOD FOR MOTHERS

GRANDMOTHER

You have loved, trained, changed diapers, Struggled

and Scarified to make us the best all around person,

we can be.

Your benefits of all your sacrifice I hope have

made you happy.

Now a second Generatlon has been born, which reminds

you daily of your earlier days of MOTHERHOOD.

You share your experiences, love, and always try to

do all you can for your "GRANDS".

You are well "loved and Respected", you have earned

being the ANGEL you are.

Kindness

Have you done a good deed today,
To help someone on their way
A cheery good morning or how are you,
Will make you feel much better too
Have a smile for every one,
That's a deed that's easily done
Kind words help others if they are in tears,
A friendly pat banishes worries and fears
Kindness turneth away wrath and doubt,
Help to erase pains within or without
Start each day with God for your guide,
His spiritual help with you will abide
When his love fills your heart,
You can give someone else a part
When you wear a smile and not a frown,
You'll gain more stars for your crown
Ask for more wisdom when you pray,
To be a blessing to someone each day
The kindness and love to others your given,
Laurels are waiting for you up in Heaven....
--Ron Francis

As Published by
The National Library of Poetry

22

Dear Dad

Thank you for Being the Father you were

Thank you for Being there for me

Thank you teaching how to dress and grooming

Thank you for teaching me there are actions and there consequences

Thank you for teaching me how to drive

Thank you for teaching me responsibilities

Thank you teaching me, to be the man I am

Letter to our Youth

Can you tell me why we cannot walk the streets in peace?

Can you tell me why children and young people are dying for no reason?

Can you tell me why children, women, and seniors are being preyed upon?

How many Mothers have to sit with tears in their eyes, how many Fathers carry broken hearts and Families Torn apart and friends with revenge on their lips?

How many young people have to become a number and statistics regarding prison inmates and head counts?

We are tired of seeing on the news that our streets are covered and stained with blood.

Yellow tape marking where their bodies laid and where they took their last breathe.

These are young people who have never had a chance to live their life or fulfill their dreams.

What are these violent acts attributed to? Is it young men who have disagreements, territory disputes, insults, disrespect, or the power that is felt?

Why does the long line of victims continue to grow year after year, and adding more names to list of senseless deaths.

Why is killing someone so easy; thoughtless without respect for life.

What would happen if the person lying on the ground died was your mother, father, brother, sister, daughter, son, and grandparent?

A bullet has little weight, but it carries an impact. A bullet carries destruction of dreams, hopes, expectations, heartache, and revenge.

One death destroys and effects many families such as the victim and the assailant.

A mother and father do not raise their child to become a killer or a victim.

Why commit a crime when you know the outcome; remember you are not as slick as you think.

Your regret after a crime will not soften the blow of death nor will it bring a person or persons back.

Life is not a game as you would play on a computer or machine, there is no reset button.

The decision you make can, may stick with you the rest of your life.

Everything in life there is a cause and effect.

If there a need to feel powerful or by using a weapon to join the military.

The military will train you how to use a weapon, how to be a man or woman.

It will teach you discipline, how to be responsible and skills. You can travel and see places you never thought you would see.

Stop and think before you react.

Focus on bringing out all the possibilities and the best within yourself.

Reveal your potential.

Printed in the United States
by Baker & Taylor Publisher Services